GUARDIANS:

A Self-Help Workbook for Child Abuse Prevention

Danny N. Liles

ABSTRACT

The purpose of *Guardians for Child Sexual Abuse Prevention and Support: A Self- Directed Workbook for Parents and Professionals* is to create a resource for parents and professionals who have limited time and access to educational materials on child sexual abuse (CSA). Hereafter, *Guardians for Child Sexual Abuse Prevention and Support: A SelfDirected Workbook for Parents and Professionals* is referred to as *Guardians*. In addition, *Guardians* aims to provide CSA information through educative material that is self-directed and adaptable to the life of the user. *Guardians'* mission is to increase CSA awareness within families and agencies in the hopes that preventative approaches to child protection are implemented in a multitude of areas within society.

Objectives for *Guardians* include the introduction of CSA, its definition, recognition of warning signs and symptoms of abuse, addressing myths and truths on CSA, awareness of child sexual offenders and grooming tactics, information on the need for medical and mental health support for survivors and their families, and heightening feelings of empowerment and advocacy for CSA prevention and intervention. Preceding the *Guardians* workbook are chapters that include the literature review, methodology for the workbook's self-directed design, and recommendations for further research, policy, and advocacy in line with the *National Association of Social Workers Code of Ethi*

Contents

CHAPTER 1

INTRODUCTION

Statement of the Problem

Childhood sexual abuse (CSA) is a taboo and obscure realm of abuse that often occurs behind closed doors and typically by those known to the children (Lanning, 2010). Indicators can be easily hidden and internalized due to the shame and harm they physically, emotionally, and mentally inflict on children (Wallis & Woodworth, 2020). CSA varies in type from disrobing children for the gratification of adults to rape. CSA impacts multiple aspects of the lives of children, other family members, and those who are identified as abusers (Rycus & Hughes, 1998). Victimization risk factors include past or concurrent forms of abuse in families and parental histories of childhood abuse victimization (Assink et al., 2019).

CSA statistics reflect the magnitude of its impact on children's lives. According to the

National Sexual Assault Hotline (Rape Abuse and Incest National Network [RAINN], 2021),

60,000 children were victims of "substantiated" or

"indicated" sexual abuse within the United States, with a

substantiated case occurring every 9 minutes annually.

CSA is, however, not the most prevalent form of abuse; in

California, for example, it is 10.0% of reported cases of

abuse (California Child Welfare Indicators Project, 2021).

Due to the nature of this form of abuse, accurate numbers

may be misconstrued, with specific populations being more

susceptible to under-or over-representation based on state

and ethnicity or race (Luken et al., 2021). According to the

pioneer work of Rycus and Hughes (1998), the nature of

CSA also contributes to these numbers, as individuals who

abuse children sexually often offend compulsively, with

repetitive behaviors building in severity over some time.

Sexual abuse of children is most likely committed by a family member or acquaintance, with 93% of survivors reporting knowing the sexual abuser (RAINN, 2015). Studies that examined the relationship between sexual abusers and survivors also reflected similar findings, with 62% of children reporting knowing their abuser (Tumbev et al., 2021). This data does not necessarily mean that all parents should be suspicious of family members or acquaintances.

Rather, it highlights the opportunistic nature of CSA and sexual abuser profiles (Winters et al., 2020). Literature dates back to the 1990s indicating that child sexual abusers have no specific demographic-with no discrimination to gender, socioeconomic status (SES), age, marital status, career choice, sexual orientation, cultural background, religious orientation, and more (Murphy

& Peters 1992). Sexual abusers of children may appear typical and "normal," posing no immediately recognizable signs of their ill intent (Lanning, 2010). Others may present as "nice guys" or "pillars of the community," complicating the public's judgment on the validity of sexual abuse allegations (Lanning, 2010, p. 23).

The impact of sexual abuse on children is considerable when assessing the emotional and prolonged effect it has on everyone involved. When assessing the critical points of recovery across the life course for survivors, "triggers," now known as "trauma reminders" (Williams & Pasztor, 2023), can occur randomly throughout their lifespan (e.g., breastfeeding, childcare, mental health, etc.; Briggs et al., 2023). Survivors of CSA also have a higher likelihood of experiencing re-victimization later in life (Papalia et al., 2021). A meta-analysis by Walker et al. (2019) reported that more than 12,000 CSA survivors reported a lifetime sexual revictimization of around 47.9%.

There are myths and misconceptions about CSA that must be addressed for prevention and support. These include minimizations or exaggerations on the extent of harm CSA poses, diffusions of perpetrator blame, denials of the extent of CSA, and perpetrator stereotypes (Cromer & Goldsmith, 2010). Many parents lack access to CSA prevention programs or feel the impact of social stigma when discussing the topic of sexuality and CSA with their children (Prikhidko & Kenny, 2021).

Purpose of the Project

The purpose of this project was to create *Guardians for Child Sexual Abuse Prevention and Support: A Self-directed Workbook for Parents and Professionals.* The aim is for parents to have a resource they can use with their kindergarten through middle school-aged children on an as-needed basis. The objectives are to:

1. Have a definition of childhood sexual abuse (CSA).

2. Recognize verbal and non-verbal warning signs and symptoms.

3. Know relevant facts and common myths.

4. Be aware of grooming and predatory cycles of possible abusers that help know when and how to talk with children about safety.

5. Know when to get medical and mental health support for children, parents, and all family members as needed.

6. Feel empowered to advocate for CSA prevention and intervention, recognizing economic, educational, and cultural considerations.

Definition of Terms

Childhood sexual abuse encompasses an array of words and expressions in policy and practice. The major definitions for this guidebook include:

Child: Every human being below the age of 18 years unless under the law applicable to the child (International Centre for Missing & Exploited Children, 2023).

Childhood sexual abuse (CSA): Contacts or interactions between a child and an adult in which the child is used for the sexual stimulation of the perpetrator or another person. Sexual abuse may also be committed by a person under the age of 18 when that person is either significantly older than the victim or is in a position of power or control over another child (Rycus & Hughes, 1998).

Non-offending parent: A parent of a child impacted by CSA who did not engage in the abuse but may have known of and failed to stop it (Rycus & Hughes, 1998).

Predator: Commensurate with person-first language, this word is being replaced with individuals who engage in sexual abuse or exploitation of children (Child Welfare Information Gateway, 2023).

Foster parent/resource parent: Used interchangeably, foster parents or resource parents are individuals or couples who are licensed, certified, or approved by public or private child welfare agencies to provide round-the-clock safety and well-being for children in their care; as resource parents they are expected to be team members in child protection and traumainformed care of children (Williams et al., 2021).

Self-directed learning: Offers individuals the opportunity to take the initiative and responsibility for their own learning and goals, typically through workbooks or guidebooks (Loeng, 2020).

Trauma reminders: Replace the word "trigger" to avoid a reference to guns (Williams & Pasztor, 2023).

Relevance to Social Work and Equity, Diversity, and Inclusion

The National Association of Social Workers (NASW; 2021) has a *Code of Ethics*, which includes six principles: service, dignity and worth of a person, importance of relationships, competence, integrity and self-care, and social justice. The NASW *Code of Ethics* relates directly to families served in the social welfare system, including children and families impacted by CSA. *Guardians for Child Sexual Abuse: Prevention and Support* embodies service as it aims to be a resource for parents. It also can be distributed to and by other agencies, organizations, and families to spread awareness.

Dignity and worth of the person is a fundamental right in not only the realm of social work but within the larger society. Many aspects create obstacles to the equal treatment of all people such as ethnicity/culture or SES.

Regardless of background, the fundamental truth is that children are a part of one of the most vulnerable populations within our society, as often, they lack the ability to self-advocate and voice concerns over wellbeing (Bagattini, 2019). *Guardians for Child Sexual Abuse: Prevention and Support* reinforces the dignity and worth of children and families who are faced with CSA. The workbook respects the importance of relationships as it unifies parents, children, and organizations in reinforcing and introducing protective factors for CSA prevention and intervention. Competence is relevant as the workbook also aims to provide educational information and additional resources for families impacted by CSA.

Integrity and self-care are integral to the recovery of CSA survivors and their families, who jointly embark on a healing journey. *Guardians* embodies the practice of implementing self- care and restoring power to survivors by sharing educational resources. The sixth objective of the workbook connects with social justice. It recognizes the disproportionate allocation of resources, addressing the lack of access parents have to CSA prevention programs (Prikhidko & Kenny, 2021). *Guardians* aims to be an accessible resource for families of all backgrounds. In addition, it also is hoped that *Guardians* can help deconstruct misconstrued public understanding of CSA and the stigma surrounding familial discussions of CSA prevention and intervention.

CHAPTER 2

LITERATURE REVIEW

The literature review is organized into the following three sections. The first section describes the characteristics and practices of both adults and juveniles who sexually abuse children. The second section addresses the impact sexual abuse has on children, including the feelings and behaviors that parents should be aware of indicating the possibility of that trauma. This section also overviews the emotional and physical impact of CSA on parents and family members, as well as abusers. The multidimensional aspects of CSA are also identified. The third section addresses the healing journey that children and family members need, as well as the help that may be given to individuals who are sexually abused. Access to possible resources and support is included. The healing journey importantly emphasizes the essential role of parents, social workers, teachers, clergy, clinicians, and advocates.

Individuals Who Sexually Abuse Children: Characteristics and Practices

The characteristics and practices of adults who sexually abuse children are challenging to describe because of the diversity of those dynamics, factors, variables, and whether the abusers are adults or adolescents. It is essential to understand common characteristics and practices of adults and younger people who have sexual attraction to children to increase awareness on potential risk factors.

Characteristics: Adults

According to the pioneering work of Murphy and Peters (1992) individuals who sexually abuse children come from an array of backgrounds. They are not representative of a particular race, ethnicity, culture, age, gender, sexual orientation and expression, marital status, or religious affiliation. They are not connected to a particular socioeconomic status, education, or

occupation (Lanning, 2010). There is research regarding psychopathological profiles for individuals with a sexual interest in children demonstrating associations with high neuroticism, possible antisocial behavior, low extraversion, and low agreeableness (Becerra-García et al., 2013). They also may experience cognitive distortion, including maladaptive beliefs or thinking, and low cognitive empathy (Lim et al., 2021).

Typologies vary in the complex subject of sexual attraction to children, but common uniformity is the sexually driven motivation or attraction to minors (Lim et al., 2021). The American Psychiatric Association (APA; 2022) defines pedophilia as a form of paraphilic disorder. This includes recurrent, intense, sexually arousing fantasies, urges, or behaviors that are distressing or disabling in relation to nonconsenting individuals, inanimate objects, or children over at least 6 months. Pedophilia is specific to the sexual attraction to prepubescent children, although the Diagnostic and Statistical Manual of Mental Disorders, Fifth Edition, Text Revision (DSM-5 TR) acknowledges that the guideline of 13 years of age and younger is an approximate age as the onset of puberty varies per individual (APA, 2022). Additionally, there is a distinction between pedophiles and non-pedophilic offenders. According to the U.S. Office of Sex Offender Sentencing, Monitoring, Apprehending, Registering, and Tracking (SMART), although pedophilia may increase chances of sexual recidivism, not all offenders who engage in CSA are filed under this DSM category (Simons, 2015). The distinction between pedophilia and child sex offending is significant as only about half of all CSA are spurred by sexual preference (Gerwinn et al., 2018).

Practices and approaches by those who sexually offend may vary. Individuals who are sexually attracted to children experience 'emotional congruence' or an emotional or cognitive affinity with children. This may manifest as a preference for social interactions with children, feeling that one has more in common with children versus adults, or choosing occupationsor positions that provide access to children (APA, 2022). According to the pioneer work of Canter et al. (1998), nearly half of sexual acts against children use grooming tactics as a part of the process. Children's susceptibility to sexual abuse is often a result of a grooming process initiated by individuals who aim to fill needs that children experience as lacking, such as parental attention or affection (Winters et al., 2020). This process is primarily utilized to exploit the immaturity of children, decreasing the likelihood of disclosure, and increasing the possibility of repeated and ongoing access (Lanning, 2010). Stages of the grooming process include isolating children, developing trust, desensitizing children, coercion and more (Winters et al., 2020). The grooming process follows a gradual intrusion of boundaries by an adult, typically following an escalation of five stages (see Table 1).

Due to the apparently non-invasive beginning, grooming is difficult to identify in earlier stages and comparable to normal adult-child interactions. Jeglic et al. (2023) provided a comprehensive study on identifying "red flag child sexual abuse grooming behaviors" (p. 11). The sample size was based on self-reports from 411 and 502 adults with and without CSA history respectively. Findings were that individuals who sexually harm often select vulnerable children who have limited parental supervision. Additionally, these individuals target children with low self-esteem, psychological or behavioral struggles, and who feel lonely, isolated, needy, unloved, or unwanted. The findings built on the work of Lanning (2010) date back several decades with the FBI and other government offices. It emphasized that the absence of adult supervision provides the opportunity for groomers to build trust by encouraging rebellion and capitalizing on children's inexperience to gratify sexual wants.

TABLE 1. The Five Stages of the Grooming Process

Targeting	Individuals looking for opportunities to offend may seek certain characteristics from children. These may include children who are trusting of adults, lonely or isolated, unwanted, or unloved, have low supervision, troubled, lacking confidence or self-esteem, or children from single-mother homes.

Gaining Access	Access to children may be sought through involvement in youth-serving organizations, engaging in activities with children alone or excluding other adults, overnight stays, manipulation of the family, and isolating children from family or peers.
Trust Development	Trust may be built using charm, position within the community (i.e., good reputation or status), utilizing rewards or privileges (e.g., toys, gifts), providing substances, favoritism (e.g., "special relationship"), giving attention or affection, and more.
Desensitization	Gradual exposure to physical touching/contact or sexual material (e.g., pornography) may be introduced in this stage of the grooming process. Other tactics may include inappropriate inquiry into sexual experiences/relationships, teaching sexual education, voyeurism, self-exposure, and more
Post-Abuse Maintenance	This stage includes interactions after the abuse occurs and may involve threats, encouraging secrets, utilizing rewards, sharing that individuals

	"love" the children, persuasion of the abuse as "normal", and victim blaming to name a few.

Note: *Data for this table was retrieved from Winters et al., 2020 (pp. 860-862).*

Grooming is utilized by offenders to create a relationship in which exploitation of children's immaturity is used to satisfy adults' sexual needs. How children and family members are targeted is essential to understand, as the grooming process involves the family, especially in the situation of younger children. Offenders will target families to lower inhibitions and gain trust as a technique to gain access to children and use their hours away from family to commence the grooming process (Lanning, 2010). Offenders identify children and families primarily through the gathering of information, from that of children's hobbies, interests, and emotional needs to that of the family (i.e., economic and physical needs).

According to the pioneering work of Conte et al. (1989), offenders also have varying physical preferences, although they will similarly target friendly and open children who are close in proximity. In addition, they may target children who have been previously victimized, demonstrated a withdrawn or quiet demeanor, or had a troubled home life. The way that offenders find access to children varies with opportunity. In terms of intrafamilial abuse, a stepfather or mother may utilize marriage to gain access to children, filling a seemingly essential family role and utilizing the position as an opportunity to offend. Another example is the use of status or a profession that grants access to children, such as clergy, sport coaches, youth centers employees, Boy Scouts, and teachers (Leclerc & Cale, 2015).

It is essential to note that although the grooming process is gradual in escalation, it may not always be the goal of offenders to rape or engage in sexual intercourse.

Sexual gratification may not be the primary reason for rape

as it may be linked to offenders' feelings of power, anger,

and control (State of California Department of Justice

[DOJ], n.d.). Offenders may be inclined to engage other

forms of sexual abuse to gratify sexual impulses. According

to the early work of Rycus and Hughes (1998), there are 13

types of sexual abuse in a continuum from nonpenetrative

to penetrative as described in Table 2.

TABLE 2. Continuum of 13 Types of Child Sexual Abuse

Nudity
An offender may, for example, may walk around their home nude.
Disrobing
The offender may disrobe in front of a child, often when there are no others present.
Observation of the Child
The offender may engage in observation as a child disrobes, uses the restroom, or bathes for the purpose of their sexual stimulation.
Genital Exposure, Exhibitionism
An offender will expose themselves to the child and may encourage the touching of genitals. In addition, there may be the invitation from the offender for the child to watch pornography or the adult's sexual activity with another adult.
Kissing
An offender may initiate kissing with the child.
Fondling
An offender may fondle the child's abdomen, genital area, breasts, buttocks, or inner thighs. There may be the request to have the child do the same to the offender.
Masturbation
The offender may watch the child masturbate, or have the child watch them masturbate.
Fellatio
Oral-genital contact between a male offender and/or child.
Cunnilingus
Oral-genital contact between a female offender and/or child.
"Dry Intercourse"
Slang to describe the rubbing between two individuals' genital or private areas, the genital-rectal area, buttocks, or inner thighs.
Penetration of the Rectal Opening or Vagina by Fingers or Objects
This form of penetration includes the insertion of objects or fingers into the vaginal or anal region using either digital penetration (i.e. finger), or inanimate objects (e.g. pencils).
Penile Penetration of the Anus or Rectal Opening
This involves penetration of a male offender's penis into a child's vaginal or anal region.
Sexual Intercourse (Rape)
Sexual intercourse may include the penetration of a female child by a male offender's penis, or the insertion of a male child's penis into a female offender.

Note: *Data for this table was retrieved from Rycus and Hughes, 1998 (pp. 155-156).*

Characteristics: Juveniles

Individuals who are at least 16 years of age and at least 5 years older than the children they abuse also may be diagnosed with a pedophilic disorder (APA, 2022). Although this statement does not apply to all juvenile offenders, many pedophilic individuals begin to offend at an early age (Darkness to Light, 2017). Risk factors for juveniles who commit sexual offenses include variables such as arousal and sexual interest in younger children, elevated psychopathology scores, history of maltreatment or adverse childhood experiences, and exposure to intra-familial sexual violence. In addition, early exposure to sex, whether this be through pornography or through other means may elevate risk as well (Ryan & Otonichar, 2016).

Debates continue over the origin of sexual actions by juveniles who commit sexual offenses against peers or younger children (Johnson, 2018). Although there are age-

appropriate expressions of sexuality among children,
behavior involving developmentally intrusive, inappropriate,
or abusive acts may signal an abnormality within sexual
development. Warning signs include compulsive
masturbation (public or chronic), humiliation or degradation
of others using sexual themes, exposure, or attempted
exposure of others' genitals, watching, or possessing
sexually aggressive pornography, written or verbal sexually
explicit threats, self-harm, and initiation of sexual
conversation with significantly younger children (Johnson,
2018). The internet and social media have facilitated access
to the sharing of sexually explicit material, an easy process.
"Sexting," or the sharing of sexually explicit photos via text
messaging, may qualify as the production of child sexual
abuse material and can incur legal and social consequences
(Moritz
& Christensen, 2020).

Multi-dimensional Impact, Factors, and Dynamics

CSA is a complex form of trauma that is a violation of a person's physical, emotional, and psychological boundaries (Wolf & Prabhu, 2021). CSA is widespread: an estimated 1 in 13 boys and 1 in 4 girls are impacted (Centers for Disease Control and Prevention [CDC], n.d.). CSA extends beyond the realm of childhood with chronic and detrimental developmental impacts across the lifespan of everyone involved (Wolf & Prabhu, 2021). The amount of harm that CSA inflicts on development may negatively impact psychological states, emotional regulation, social interactions, or physical health. Children's experience of abuse creates a risk factor for symptoms of anxiety, depression, stress, and mental health problems later in life as well as in childhood (Maciel & BastoPereira, 2020). The re-establishment of trust with others and intimacy are acknowledged difficulties (Collin-Vézina et al., 2013).

Children who experienced CSA in comparison to other forms of abuse had significantly greater internalizing and externalizing issues over time (Lewis et al., 2016). One example of CSA's impact further highlights its multidimensional effect. The four factor tramagenics model suggests that CSA impacts children by altering their emotional and cognitive orientation. According to this model, trauma impacts survivors' capacity to express emotion and/or feeling, in addition to distorting their self-concept with four trauma factors: betrayal, powerlessness, stigmatization, and traumatic sexualization (Collin-Vézina et al., 2013).

Disclosure

CSA disclosure is often delayed if at all revealed. Around 86% of survivors share never reporting abuse, with 52 being the average age of CSA reporting (Child USA, 2020). Disclosure is complex as there are many factors that may influence whether children follow through with seeking help (Manay & Collin-Vézina, 2021). Often, disclosure can be contingent on culture, age, gender, intellectual ability, relationship to the perpetrator, nature of abuse, feelings of shame, fear, or embarrassment, and family function (Child USA, 2020). Intrafamilial abuse may heighten the likelihood of delayed disclosure, especially if the individuals who commit the sexual abuse live in the home of the victim (Wallis & Woodworth, 2020). Survivors attempting gradual disclosure to peers are not necessarily going to report to parents or individuals with authority (Manay & Collin-Vézina, 2021).

CSA Disclosure and Impact on Families

CSA's impact extends beyond survivors to affect those around them, including siblings, family, friends, or communities. Although this process may take years to begin, often the first awareness of abuse begins with disclosure. This has a significant impact on family systems, especially the non-offending caregiver(s). Often, there are feelings of disbelief, self-blame, denial, and distress, including clinical difficulties in response to awareness of CSA (McElvaney & Nixon, 2020). A longitudinal study following the impact of CSA on the health of mothers and fathers ($n = 124$) found that they perceived their health to have significantly worsened in the year following disclosure (Cyr et al., 2018). The impact of CSA disclosure had a main effect on their limitation of daily activities due to declining physical health and increased reports of psychological distress.

The smaller study of McElvaney and Nixon (2020) focused on the internal experience of parents, three key themes were identified by the 20 participating mothers and fathers: making sense of the abuse in retrospect, negotiating parental identity as a protector, and navigating services. When attempting to make sense of the abuse, parents questioned why their children had a delay in confiding with them by thinking back to their children's behaviors: "*I felt he (child) shoulda came when it was happening because I always told him if anybody done anything to him that wasn't right no matter what they say to him that he should tell me*" (mother of 15-year-old CSA survivor; McElvaney & Nixon, 2020, p. 1780). Parents struggled to understand their children's lack of confidence in them as protectors, contradicting their own views of themselves in that role. Therefore, child-parent relationships were altered in response, with some parents becoming hyper-protective (McElvaney & Nixon, 2020).

Parents shared similarities in their feelings of being "lost" or confused, and their difficulties in managing the post-disclosure process. If the experience also included the child welfare system and law enforcement, parents may have minimal direction and instruction on where to receive services. In addition, delayed access to services also

became an obstacle for some parents, with one father

reporting that approximately 4 months had passed before

there was contact with a social worker. Overall, although

this study had a small proportion of parents, it shadows the

cycle of grief, confusion, and obstacles parental figures

may experience post- disclosure. The impact of disclosure

may surpass emotional and psychological impacts,

extending to physical wellbeing.

CSA Indicators: Physical, Emotional, and Behaviors

One of the themes from the McElvaney and Nixon

(2020) study included parental awareness of behavioral

indicators by their children that abuse was occurring. What

behaviors to be   aware of is pivotal to

prevention as there   presence   are physical, behavioral, and

emotional indicators. Physical indicators may include injury

to the genital or rectal area (e.g., bruising, lacerations, bite marks, a stretched rectum, etc.), of sexually transmitted

diseases (e.g., herpes), suspicious stains on the

undergarments (e.g., blood), urinary or bladder infections,

painful bowel movements or encopresis (i.e., lack of bowel

control), and early pregnancy (Rycus & Hughes,

1998). Physical indicators of CSA may not always be

present, as abuse may include other lessphysically injurious

such as fondling, kissing, or groping. In those circumstances,

behavioral and emotional indicators may arise. Although

children's responses may vary, there are specific behaviors

that can signal abuse, as listed in Table 3. Types of CSA

Indicators.

TABLE 3. Types of CSA Indicators

Types of CSA Indicators
• Fear or phobias, which can include avoidance of specific individuals, genders, avoidance or fear of physical contact, sex (i.e., adolescents), or an unusual fear of specific locations.
• Aggressive behavioral shifts (i.e., tantrums, running away, fighting).

- Withdrawal from engaging in social relationships, such as with family or peers, and isolation.
- Developmentally regressive behaviors, specifically with younger children. This can include soiling (i.e. urinary or fecal), thumb sucking, head banging, clingy behavior, or rocking.
- Sleeping, eating, or hygiene disturbances. An additional aspect to consider are changes in manner of dress, such as excessively baggy clothing, which may be indicative of an attempt to protect or hide their body.
- Generalized irritability or inability to concentrate.
- Generalized anger that may be directed to him/herself or others. This may include selfinjurious behavior, unexplainable rages, inflicting harm on animals or others, etc.
- Feelings of depression or anxiety (i.e., crying easily, have a general lack of interest in surroundings or others, is withdrawn, hypervigilant, etc.).
- Inappropriate or sexual behavior. The authors clarify that children are too immature cognitively, emotionally, or socially to consent and understand their actions and traumatically conditioned sexual behavior.
- Engaging in sophisticated sexual play with peers or engaging in prostitution or promiscuity. In addition, the use of toys to create or play out sexual scenarios

that may have elements of coercion, dominance, force, or threats.

- Excessive or public masturbation.
- Involving younger peers in extensive sexual activity.
- An attempt to hide clothing that is bloodied, stained, or soiled from sexual activity.

Note: *The data for this table is from Rycus and Hughes, 1998 (pp. 164-165).*

The Healing Journey

Treatment and Recovery of CSA Survivors

The trajectory of CSA treatment is non-linear and often continuous, including a process of both acceptance of past traumas and the culmination of internal change. For example, Arias and Johnson (2013) interviewed 10 female CSA survivors, looking at their self-reported perceptions of healing. Respondents shared that important types of healing included the need for compassion and empathy, therapy, confronting abusers and holding them responsible, and participating in formal and informal education. Experiences also varied based on age, gender, type of CSA, or other individual factors, as well as treatment approaches (Arias &

Johnson,

2013).

Disclosure and the Healing Journey

It is essential to provide a healthy, trusting, and open

stream of communication between parents and children.

Disclosure probability is more likely if children are aware

of what touch or interactions are inappropriate if there is

support by peers to disclose to individuals of authority, and

access to a support system. Merely asking children what

they are going through or experiencing raises the

probability of disclosure (Brennan & McElvaney, 2020).

Many aspects of initial disclosure contribute to survivors'

healing journey. Maladaptive coping increases the chances

of lasting negative effects on survivors of CSA including

lack of support and experiences of fear and anxiety

(Watkins- Kagebein et al., 2019).

Traumatic disclosure experiences can increase the continued adverse impact of CSA, which can encompass harmful reactions toward the survivor including disbelief, anger, confusion, and more (Watkins-Kagebein et al., 2019). Optimal treatment for CSA should include elements of psychoeducation, exposure through a trauma narrative, and the presence of supportive therapeutic relationships. Safety planning and the teaching of coping skills should additionally be implemented during treatment (Shuman, 2020). Examples of such treatment include trauma-focused cognitive behavioral therapy, play therapy, art therapy, and group therapy. An overarching theme surrounding treatment is the attempt to restore feelings of expression and safety and the ability to facilitate emotional and behavioral regulation.

Therapeutic interventions for non-offending parents are similar to those interventions implemented with children.

These include, for example, support groups and mental health services in addition to navigation of services (e.g., legal, financial assistance, medical, and therapeutic (Shuman, 2020). Healing also needs to happen for other family members, including the non-offending parent, but more recent research indicates that more information is needed on their roles, the impact of socio-economic and marital statuses, and coping strategies (Vilvens et al., 2021).

CSA Awareness and Prevention Programs

Preventative education on CSA awareness has a long history regarding approaches and techniques, including the use of school-based programs (Del Campo & Fávero, 2020; Rudolph et al., 2018). Engaging parents and children in CSA education is necessary for prevention effectiveness, although it is unclear how children's ages and stages of development impact what they can understand (Kurtça, 2022; Rudolph et al., 2018). Historically, schools have been sites where CSA school-based prevention programs have been implemented (Rudolph et al., 2018). An example of a school-based program includes "good touch, bad touch." This prevention program, administered via school curriculum, teaches students personal body safety, including identifying private body areas and empowering students in saying "no" (Jeglic & Calkins, 2018).

It is crucial to note that a key reason regarding the lack of parents' educating their children on CSA may be their believing the children are not old enough to understand, or that the schools are responsible (Kurtça, 2022; Rudolph et al., 2018). This approach, however, creates opportunities for increased vulnerability to the grooming process, which often begins subtly and gradually (Jeglic et al., 2023). To effectively implement effective prevention strategies, interventions must be tailored to the developmental level of survivors (Shuman, 2020). Parents are essential in prevention programs as they are the primary resources for children in relation to physical, psychological, social, and sexual development (Kurtça, 2022).

Regarding the likelihood of peer-on-peer sexual offenses, an additional concern regarding parental roles in CSA prevention is the monitoring of children's behavior, specifically uncharacteristic sexual behavior. A misconception is that juveniles who commit sex offenses will become adult child sexual offenders (Darkness to Light, 2017). Redirection of early abnormal sexual behavior is optimal for parents who observe this behavior to minimize the risk of adult offenses (Johnson, 2018). Literature regarding prevention strategy effectiveness points to the goals of increasing knowledge (e.g., questionnaires), and acquisition of skills learned from prevention teachings (e.g., role playing, structured interviews) as main objectives (Del Campo &

Fávero, 2020).

Accessing Supports

Additional consideration for program implementation includes costs and accessibility. Where resources for families may be scarce or minimal, other professionals are needed to advocate for the availability of prevention services. Mandated reporters or those who work closely with families may also aid in CSA prevention. Mandated reporters serve in a multitude of careers and professions. Youth service organizations (YSOs), schools, places of worship, and recreational clubs, are locations where CSA prevention programs can occur. Trust in adults who provide these services may be taken for granted by parents who believe that their children are safe and are supervised from danger (Assini-Meytin et al., 2021). However, these also are locations where CSA occurs. Despite this, YSOs serve as places where a multitude of services can be made accessible to families in need.

CSA can occur in any community, and some cultures may be more or less able to address it. With cultural diversity, a particular element of 'collectivism' may emphasize individuals as a unit within their communities. Ethnically diverse communities may place high value on elements of social order, harmony, or social hierarchy (Sawrikar & Katz, 2018). Because of this, CSA may collectively impact more than the family of the survivor and extend to others within the ethnic community as well as the accessibility of resources. In addition, there may be differing beliefs as to what constitutes sexual abuse, which may influence whether parents report or address abuse (Sanjeevi et al., 2018). Considering these factors, it is essential to implement culture-conscious approaches to addressing CSA in different communities.

Individuals who Sexually Abuse and Opportunities for Healing

Treatment for those who sexually abuse children may vary and include sexual offender treatment programs. Such programs include both secondary prevention (immediate services) and tertiary or long-term prevention services (Jackson et al., 2022). In addition, social stigma may also create a boundary in access to treatment. To provide this, it is necessary that practitioners aid in specific realms of treatment. Some of this may include a practitioner's understanding of sexual offenses and those who commit sexual offenses (Wilcox, 2017). Effective treatment may include therapy in multiple aspects, such as addressing underlying mental health disorders, deviant sexual interests, and lack of empathy to name a few areas (Hanson & Yates, 2013).

Overall, continued research in this field is needed, specifically for non-offending minor attracted individuals who experience difficulties in accessing support due to stigma, fear of discovery, and of vigilantism (Jackson et al., 2022).

This chapter addressed the characteristics and practices of both adults and juveniles who sexually abuse children, the impact sexual abuse has on children and the multidimensional aspects of CSA. It also addressed "the healing journey" for children and adults impacted by CSA. This information provides the foundation for the following self-directed workbook for parents and professionals as guardians for CSA prevention and support.

CHAPTER 3

METHODOLOGY

Introduction

This chapter is divided into three sections. The first section focuses on the target population for *Guardians for Child Sexual Abuse Prevention and Support: A Selfdirected Workbook for Parents and Professionals.* The second section identifies the workbook goals and objectives. The third section details the workbook's design and format. Understanding the target populations, goals and objectives, and design and format are essential for implementing the workbook, which is described in Chapter 4.

The workbook itself is included in the Appendix of this publication. Going forward,

Guardians will be used instead of the full name.

Target Population

Guardians aims to aid parents of children in kindergarten through middle school in educating them on intervention strategies against CSA. Parents can be inclusive of foster and adoptive parents, kinship caregivers, and any family structure. *Guardians* provides the necessary tools to educate parents and their children regarding the vulnerabilities and risk factors that heighten the chances of CSA victimization. It is designed to include all genders, gender identities, sexual expression, and CSA histories.

An additional target population is social work professionals who work at public and non-profit child welfare agencies, advocacy centers, and organizations. All individuals who are mandated reporters, including teachers, clinicians, and clergy may utilize this workbook to implement in their respective fields while in service to families.

Workbook Goals and Objectives

The aim is to create a resource regarding CSA, especially prevention and intervention strategies. *Guardians* also explains potential behavioral shifts within children that may indicate abuse. In addition, this workbook provides resources for continued healing.

The specific objectives are to:

1. Have a definition of childhood sexual abuse (CSA).

2. Recognize verbal and non-verbal signs and symptoms or warning signs.

3. Acknowledge common myths and facts.

4. Be aware of grooming and predatory cycles of possible abusers that considers when and how to talk with children about safety.

5. Know when to get medical and mental health support for children, parents, and all family members as needed.

6. Feel empowered to advocate for CSA prevention and intervention, recognizing economic, educational, and cultural considerations.

Design and Format

Guardians is designed as a self-directed resource. 'Self-directed' defines a person taking the initiative, with or without assistance, in their learning experience, formulating learning goals, choosing and implementing learning strategies, identifying human and material resources for learning, and evaluating learning resources (Knowles, 1975). The rationale is to be respectful of families' diverse backgrounds, lifestyles, work schedules, and other commitments. In addition, *Guardians* considers the constricting timeframes parents and professionals may have. This way, they can take advantage of all that the workbook offers without being constrained by set times and locations required with group training.

Parents typically are the greatest influences in their children's lives. From a positive perspective, this role is most optimal in discussion of CSA risks, prevention, and their ability to create safe environments for their children's confidence development. Parental discussions surrounding CSA are effective when specific abuse behaviors are covered, such as identities of perpetrators, inappropriate touching, and hypothetical abuse scenarios and responses to abuse (Rudolph et al., 2018).

Alternatively, parents may also have a negative impact. In dynamics where a parent is the perpetrator of CSA, there is an additional barrier to child protection due to the intrafamilial type of harm being inflicted. In some families, a parent may not be the abuser but can be what has been identified as "the non-offending parent" (Rycus & Hughes, 1998). When abuse is ., *Guardians* disclosed or discovered by non-offending parents, there can be a variety of responses like confusion or fear on how to proceed with caring for their children. Advocates, social workers, and other mandated reporters must be prepared to aid nonoffending parents by providing services and resources (e.g).

The format of this workbook provides parents with the flexibility to structure discussions with their children about CSA. As CSA is a difficult topic to discuss, it is essential to provide parents with opportunities to discuss with their children according to their ages, developmental milestones, and circumstances. The format additionally provides parents and professionals with the content to cover, which, in turn, may strengthen their own knowledge on CSA prevention, risk factors, and interventions. The workbook format also provides the opportunity for sharing among individuals, families, groups, agencies, and organizations.

The format includes a title and copyright page, acknowledgements, table of contents, the e., myth goals, and objectives, and all the supporting activities. These include, for example, fact sheets (i. vs. fact on CSA), scenarios/vignettes, critical thinking sections, and references (including Internet resources). Activities are designed to be user- friendly and written at a level of understanding appropriate for a wide array of parents, families, and professionals. *Guardians* also is designed to be respectful of individuals who use/read English as a second language. *Guardians* también está diseñado para ser respetuoso con las personas que usan o leen inglés como segundo idioma.

In summary, *Guardians for Child Sexual Abuse Prevention and Support: A Self- directed Workbook for Parents and Professionals* aims to provide the supports for all adults responsible for recognizing and preventing childhood victimization.

CHAPTER 4

THE WORKBOOK

Introduction

This chapter is divided into four sections that address workbook implementation. The first section outlines how to utilize this workbook and additional materials needed that can assist in using it productively. The second section highlights propositions addressing the benefits of the workbook. The third section provides recommendations for sharing the workbook and parent engagement for CSA prevention. Additionally, the fourth section overviews evaluation strategies for assessment of workbook impact.

How to Use the Workbook

Guardians for Child Sexual Abuse is a self-instructional workbook that highlights its ability to be a take-home, versatile, and adaptable resource to heighten CSA awareness. *Guardians for Child Sexual Abuse* will be a valuable resource to parents who aim to heighten both their own and their children's awareness of CSA risk factors, correction of false CSA beliefs, and the implementation of prevention strategies. This workbook will include guidance on how to utilize provided resources, which will be in the Appendix. To provide and create a user-friendly workbook accessible to all families regardless of access to the entire book, it will be formatted with instructions included. Instructions will be found within the workbook, followed by the title page, acknowledgements, table of contents/ activities page, rationale page, and the purpose statement, including goals and objectives

Materials Needed

Required materials that may be needed to complete the workbook can include a pen, pencil, or highlighter for participants to write notes, highlight key information, or complete activities. The workbook will be organized in a binder in preparation for any additional additions to the complied resource materials. Additional supplementary materials (i.e., computer with internet access) may be needed to access online materials although this is not required to have for workbook usage. Resource pages will include notifications on alternative access, which may include direction to libraries or outside agency materials.

Engaging Participants

The workbook focuses on engaging both parents and resource families who are in the care of kindergarten through middle school-aged children. Participants may be recognized through foster care agencies, child welfare agencies, support groups, school institutions, and/or religious institutions. Copies of the workbook may be offered as a resource to families or agencies that are interested. Provided below are two vignettes highlighting how *Guardians* could be offered to families:

Scenario 1

5-year-old Lain has been to see a primary care provider almost weekly for the past month. Lain has complained to her mother, Tina, that her stomach hurts. Tina, in response to her daughter's claim, takes Lain to her physician to be examined. Carmen, Lain's physician, notes that her only symptom is abdominal pain with no nausea, vomiting, or diarrhea present. Carmen finds that Lain is otherwise a healthy child and well-cared for. Multiple diagnostic tests were conducted, and Carmen discovered a test result indicating Lain had tested positive for syphilis, a sexually transmitted infection (STI). As the family nurse practitioner, Carmen informs Tina that Lain has tested positive for syphilis. Tina, distraught at the news, is in disbelief and confused as to what to do next. Carmen, knowledgeable on the signs of CSA, provides Tina with treatment for her daughter, along with *Guardians*.

Scenario 2

Sam is stepmother to 6-year-old Charly and has been married to his father, Tom, for the last 12 months. Sam has been concerned with Tom's controlling nature since the beginning of their relationship. Sam has held some concern over Tom and Charly's relationship, as she believes it is too close of a father-and-son relationship. Sam has observed that Tom is overprotective of Charly, not allowing him to play with other children when he is over at their home, and even limiting Charly's time with Sam. Sam has shared with her therapist the concern that Tom may be sexually abusing Charly. Sam provided some examples that contributed to her suspicions, such as seeing Tom leave Charly's room early in the morning and witnessing him throwing a used condom in the trash. Sam is unsure whether her concerns are valid, or if she is 'over-reacting' due to her history with abuse. Sam's therapist provides her with *Guardians* as a take-home resource and advises Sam to report her concerns to the child abuse hotline, which is located within the workbook.

Evaluation

Considering that *Guardians* is a self-instructional workbook that may be utilized by all families and/or organizations, there is no concreate opportunity to receive feedback of its effectiveness. However, a self-administered review is within the workbook to provide users a reflection on how it assisted them. The following questions may be provided:

1. "In what ways was *Guardians* content (information shared) useful?"

2. "Has *Guardians* and its format aided in your understanding of CSA and its prevention?"

3. "How likely would you be in sharing *Guardians* with other parents and/or professionals?"

A Likert scale will be implemented with a 1 to 3 range in connection to question 3, with 1 being *not likely*, 2 being *likely*, and 3 being *very likely*. Outside agencies who wish to utilize the workbook may hire an evaluator if additional assessment is needed to measure how impactful it was.

CHAPTER 5

CONCLUSION

This chapter builds on the previous four chapters in preparation for the *Workbook* located in the Appendix. Divided into four sections, the chapter reviews the goal and objectives of the

Guardians for Child Sexual Abuse Prevention: A Workbook for Parents and Professionals

(hereafter referred to as *Guardians)*; identifies the Workbook's strengths and limitations; discusses implications for social work policy, practice, research, and advocacy; and shares lessons learned through the process of developing *Guardians* for this California State University, Long Beach School of Social Work, Master of Social Work (MSW) book project. Going forward, child sexual abuse is referred to as CSA.

Goal and Objectives

The purpose of this self-directed workbook, *Guardians,* is to create a resource for all parents who could benefit from basic knowledge with skills and resources to provide care and protection of kindergarten through middle school-aged children on an as-needed basis. "Parents" can include foster or resource parents, kinship caregivers, and adoptive parents. Professionals can include child welfare and mental health social workers, counselors or therapists, teachers, and clergy.

Guardian's self-directed instructional activities are developed to be used independently from in-person training to provide diversity in use. In addition, the challenging topic of CSA provides both parents and professionals with the opportunity to structure their own learning around busy schedules or self-paced preferences. *Guardians* is created to be accessible to a wide variety of individuals who may not have access to this format of instructional material. By completing *Guardians*, it is the hope of the developer that *Guardians* will provide parents and professionals with the awareness, knowledge, skills and resources to recognize CSA, and provide whatever prevention and interventions will be most beneficial.

Workbook Strengths and Limitations

Guardian's self-directed design is a strength. The day-to-day lives of parents and professionals often is filled with numerous caregiving tasks and workplace responsibilities. Varying schedules leave little time to participate in both basic and intensive training on CSA. Therefore, *Guardian*'s information and activities share information on CSA that can be adapted as needed. The intense and recognizable difficulty of *Guardians* is reflected in the way the developer presented the information. Through its self-directional design, individuals using *Guardians* have the opportunity to choose what topics to cover and at a pace that is comfortable either independently or with others.

Most importantly, the design provides a safe space to learn

basics about CSA or build on previous knowledge.

> A limitation of *Guardians* is the vast amount of
> information that could not be included.

Although the workbook is created to assist in acquiring

knowledge on CSA, the content may not be applicable to

all circumstances. Reactions or indicators of CSA vary by

individuals, environments, or abuser-victim dynamics.

There also is diversity in child sexual offender typologies,

which also vary in age, ethnicity, gender, sexual

orientation, profession, and background (Lim et al., 2021).

Another limitation was the decision to focus on CSA

relating to children between the ages of kindergarten

through middle school, as issues regarding juvenile sexual

offenders would require more content than this workbook

could provide. Lastly, interventions and treatment options

related to sexual offenders and their rehabilitation post-abuse is not within the scope of this workbook.

While the self-directed format is a strength, it also can be a limitation. Self-directed learning is the responsibility of the users. *Guardians* endeavors to be culturally sensitive however, its English-only format may not be sufficiently helpful to other speakers. Further, the time frames of *Guardians* as the MSW book project limited the amount of information that could be covered and its format. Lastly, while the information shared within *Guardians* is based on peer-reviewed literature, the workbook itself has not been tested for reliability or validity.

Implications for Social Work Policy, Practice, Research, and Advocacy

The need for a resource such as Guardians is significant. According to RAINN (2021) 60,000 children were victims of "substantiated" or "indicated" sexual abuse within the United

States in the year 2021. RAINN substantiate that CSA occurs every 9 minutes annually. Further, 93% of these children know their abuser (RAINN, 2015). Although these numbers indicate a high rate of abuse, CSA accounts for only 10% of California's reported cases of child abuse (California Child Welfare Indicators Project, 2021). It has been said that statistics are human beings with the tears washed away (McPherson & Blazucki, 2023). Both on a national and state level, there is a compelling need to address CSA for both parents and professionals.

The disclosure of CSA often begins with the voice of a child and the investigative procedure of the mandated reporter. From the moment of disclosure, the responsibility of protective action is passed to mandated reporters who assume the role of guardians in securing the safety of a CSA survivor (Peace Officer Standards and Training [POST], 2021).

However, investigation of CSA often occurs after children have been harmed. Therefore, it is necessary for child welfare services to prioritize prevention strategies and psychoeducation when working with families to prevent abuse. In line with this logic, it is necessary to implement and advocate for self-instructional prevention strategies.

Guardians embodies this goal, as the workbook material begins the difficult discussion of what CSA is. Conversations on CSA prior to its occurrence can aid families and professionals in formulating prevention strategies, in addition to beginning their own discussions with their children on CSA awareness. *Guardians* aims to correct misconstrued understanding of CSA, and the stigma surrounding familial discussions of CSA prevention and intervention.

Lessons Learned

The decision to learn more about CSA and share that learning with others who could make a difference with their knowledge began at the start of the MSW book course. Given the opportunity to create a self-instructional workbook, the vision for *Guardians* began to unfold. The literature review provided ample information regarding the longitudinal impact of CSA on survivors from a multitude of viewpoints which included physical, mental, emotional, and spiritual topics. Current literature covered a large portion of adult survivors and their resilience and coping behaviors after surviving their abuse. Although the impact of CSA was evident, there were limited options for research in the realm of non-offending parental experiences and the implementation of prevention programs. Further exploration into CSA resulted in the inquiry of the sexual offender and a lack of studies surrounding why they offend. It was concerning to the developer to discover the true scale of CSA offenses and the misappropriated caution attributed to "strangers" rather than the statistically relevant "known" sexual offender. In consideration of the research, in addition to national and statewide statistics on CSA, the development of the workbook aimed to address the gaps in literature. *Guardians* aims to facilitate conversations that target key aspects of CSA victimization, covering child risk factors, parental responsibility, and offender profiles.

The actual development of *Guardians* was a second area of learning. A challenge previously covered in the limitations included the vast information surrounding CSA. As a result of the research, it was the goal of the developer to create activities that introduced CSA topics for parents and professionals in a user-friendly way. To prevent an overload of information, and limit the scope of research, the workbook approached CSA education in a simpler, introductory manner. This choice aimed to create a workbook that could be accessible to individuals of all levels of CSA knowledge and education. The literature review required organizational and time management skills to cover extensive areas of studies, including pre- and post-abuse experiences, offender typology research, and more intense areas of research. Weekly consultations with the book advisor aided in the formulation of workbook activities, goals, and objectives in addition to inspiring motivation and creativity in *Guardians'* development. The creation of *Guardians*, from the conception of an idea to the fruition of a workbook, heightened the developer's knowledge on CSA peer-reviewed literature and awareness of a necessity for CSA prevention advocacy. Through the process, *Guardians* reflects and respects the NASW major principles: helping parents and professionals be more competent, ensuring the dignity and worth of children, supporting relationships, providing service and essentially, being an advocate for the social justice that all children deserve.